The Buller-Podington Compact

By

Frank Richard Stockton

[ZHINGOORA BOOKS]

THE BULLER-PODINGTON COMPACT

"I tell you, William," said Thomas Buller to his friend Mr. Podington, "I am truly sorry about it, but I cannot arrange for it this year. Now, as to *my* invitation—that is very different."

"Of course it is different," was the reply, "but I am obliged to say, as I said before, that I really cannot accept it."

Remarks similar to these had been made by Thomas Buller and William Podington at least once a year for some five years. They were old friends; they had been schoolboys together and had been associated in business since they were young men. They had now reached a vigorous middle age; they were each married, and each had a house in the country in which he resided for a part of the year. They were warmly attached to each other, and each was the best friend which the other had in this world. But during all these years neither of them had visited the other in his country home.

The reason for this avoidance of each other at their respective rural residences may be briefly stated. Mr. Buller's country house was situated by the sea, and he was very fond of the water. He had a good cat-boat, which he sailed himself with much judgment and skill, and it was his greatest pleasure to take his friends and visitors upon little excursions on the bay. But Mr. Podington was desperately afraid of the water, and he was particularly afraid of any craft sailed by an amateur. If his friend Buller would have employed a professional mariner, of years and experience, to steer and manage his boat, Podington might have been willing to take an occasional sail; but as Buller always insisted upon sailing his own boat, and took it ill if any of his visitors doubted his ability to do so properly, Podington did not wish to wound the self-love of his friend, and he did not wish to be drowned. Consequently he could not bring himself to consent to go to Buller's house by the sea.

To receive his good friend Buller at his own house in the beautiful upland region in which he lived would have been a great joy to Mr. Podington; but Buller could not be induced to visit him. Podington was very fond of horses and always drove himself, while Buller was more afraid of horses than he was of elephants or lions. To one or more horses driven by a coachman of years and experience he did not always object, but to a horse driven by Podington, who had much experience and knowledge regarding mercantile affairs, but was merely an amateur horseman, he most decidedly and strongly objected. He did not wish to hurt his friend's feelings by refusing to go out to drive with him, but he would not rack his own nervous system by accompanying him. Therefore it was that he had not yet visited the beautiful upland country residence of Mr. Podington.

At last this state of things grew awkward. Mrs. Buller and Mrs. Podington, often with their families, visited each other at their country houses, but the fact that on these occasions they were never accompanied by their husbands caused more and more gossip among their neighbors both in the upland country and by the sea.

One day in spring as the two sat in their city office, where Mr. Podington had just repeated his annual invitation, his friend replied to him thus:

"William, if I come to see you this summer, will you visit me? The thing is beginning to look a little ridiculous, and people are talking about it."

Mr. Podington put his hand to his brow and for a few moments closed his eyes. In his mind he saw a cat-boat upon its side, the sails spread out over the water, and two men, almost entirely immersed in the waves, making efforts to reach the side of the boat. One of these was getting on very well—that was Buller. The other seemed about to sink, his arms were uselessly waving in the air—that was himself. But he opened his eyes and looked bravely out of the window; it was time to conquer all this; it was indeed growing ridiculous. Buller had been sailing many years and had never been upset.

"Yes," said he; "I will do it; I am ready any time you name."

Mr. Buller rose and stretched out his hand.

"Good!" said he; "it is a compact!"

Buller was the first to make the promised country visit. He had not mentioned the subject of horses to his friend, but he knew through Mrs. Buller that Podington still continued to be his own driver. She had informed him, however, that at present he was accustomed to drive a big black horse which, in her opinion, was as gentle and reliable as these animals ever became, and she could not imagine how anybody could be afraid of him. So when, the next morning after his arrival, Mr. Buller was asked by his host if he would like to take a drive, he suppressed a certain rising emotion and said that it would please him very much.

When the good black horse had jogged along a pleasant road for half an hour Mr. Buller began to feel that, perhaps, for all these years he had been laboring under a misconception. It seemed to be possible that there were some horses to which surrounding circumstances in the shape of sights and sounds were so irrelevant that they were to a certain degree entirely safe, even when guided and controlled by an amateur hand. As they passed some meadow-land, somebody behind a hedge fired a gun; Mr. Buller was frightened, but the horse was not.

"William," said Buller, looking cheerfully around him,

"I had no idea that you lived in such a pretty country. In fact, I might almost call it beautiful. You have not any wide stretch of water, such as I like so much, but here is a pretty river, those rolling hills are very charming, and, beyond, you have the blue of the mountains."

"It is lovely," said his friend; "I never get tired of driving through this country. Of course the seaside is very fine, but here we have such a variety of scenery."

Mr. Buller could not help thinking that sometimes the seaside was a little monotonous, and that he had lost a great deal of pleasure by not varying his summers by going up to spend a week or two with Podington.

"William," said he, "how long have you had this horse?"

"About two years," said Mr. Podington; "before I got him, I used to drive a pair."

"Heavens!" thought Buller, "how lucky I was not to come two years ago!" And his regrets for not sooner visiting his friend greatly decreased.

Now they came to a place where the stream, by which the road ran, had been dammed for a mill and had widened into a beautiful pond.

"There now!" cried Mr. Buller. "That's what I like. William, you seem to have everything! This is really a very pretty sheet of water, and the reflections of the trees over there make a charming picture; you can't get that at the seaside, you know."

Mr. Podington was delighted; his face glowed; he was rejoiced at the pleasure of his friend. "I tell you, Thomas," said he, "that——"

"William!" exclaimed Buller, with a sudden squirm in his seat, "what is that I hear? Is that a train?"

"Yes," said Mr. Podington, "that is the ten-forty, up."

"Does it come near here?" asked Mr. Buller, nervously. "Does it go over that bridge?"

"Yes," said Podington, "but it can't hurt us, for our road goes under the bridge; we are perfectly safe; there is no risk of accident."

"But your horse! Your horse!" exclaimed Buller, as the train came nearer and nearer. "What will he do?"

"Do?" said Podington; "he'll do what he is doing now; he doesn't mind trains."

"But look here, William," exclaimed Buller, "it will get there just as we do; no horse could stand a roaring up in the air like that!"

Podington laughed. "He would not mind it in the least," said he.

"Come, come now," cried Buller. "Really, I can't stand this! Just stop a minute, William, and let me get out. It sets all my nerves quivering."

Mr. Podington smiled with a superior smile. "Oh, you needn't get out," said he; "there's not the least danger in the world. But I don't want to make you nervous, and I will turn around and drive the other way."

"But you can't!" screamed Buller. "This road is not wide enough, and that train is nearly here. Please stop!"

The imputation that the road was not wide enough for him to turn was too much for Mr. Podington to bear. He was very proud of his ability to turn a vehicle in a narrow place.

"Turn!" said he; "that's the easiest thing in the world. See; a little to the right, then a back, then a sweep to the left and we will be going the other way." And instantly he began the maneuver in which he was such an adept.

"Oh, Thomas!" cried Buller, half rising in his seat, "that train is almost here!"

"And we are almost——" Mr. Podington was about to say "turned around," but he stopped. Mr. Buller's exclamations had made him a little nervous, and, in his anxiety to turn quickly, he had pulled upon his horse's bit with more energy than was actually necessary, and his nervousness being communicated to the horse, that animal backed with such extraordinary vigor that the hind wheels of the wagon went over a bit of grass by the road and into the water. The sudden jolt gave a new impetus to Mr. Buller's fears.

"You'll upset!" he cried, and not thinking of what he was about, he laid hold of his friend's arm. The horse, startled by this sudden jerk upon his bit, which, combined with the thundering of the train, which was now on the bridge, made him think that something extraordinary was about to happen, gave a sudden and forcible start backward, so that not only the hind wheels of the light wagon, but the fore wheels and his own hind legs went into the water. As the bank at this spot sloped steeply, the wagon continued to go backward, despite the efforts of the agitated horse to find a footing on the crumbling edge of the bank.

"Whoa!" cried Mr. Buller.

"Get up!" exclaimed Mr. Podington, applying his whip upon the plunging beast.

But exclamations and castigations had no effect upon the horse. The original bed of the stream ran close to the road, and the bank was so steep and the earth so soft that it was impossible for the horse to advance or even maintain his footing. Back, back he went, until the whole equipage was in the water and the wagon was afloat.

This vehicle was a road wagon, without a top, and the joints of its box-body were tight enough to prevent the water from immediately entering it; so, somewhat deeply sunken, it rested upon the water. There was a current in this part of the pond and it turned the wagon downstream. The horse was now entirely immersed in the water, with the exception of his head and the upper part of his neck, and, unable to reach the bottom with his feet, he made vigorous efforts to swim.

Mr. Podington, the reins and whip in his hands, sat horrified and pale; the accident was so sudden, he was so startled and so frightened that, for a moment, he could not speak a word. Mr. Buller, on the other hand, was now lively and alert. The wagon had no sooner floated away from the shore than he felt himself at home. He was upon his favorite element; water had no fears for him. He saw that his friend was nearly frightened out of his wits, and that, figuratively speaking, he must step to the helm and take charge of the vessel. He stood up and gazed about him.

"Put her across stream!" he shouted; "she can't make headway against this current. Head her to that clump of trees on the other side; the bank is lower there, and we can beach her. Move a little the other way, we must trim boat. Now then, pull on your starboard rein."

Podington obeyed, and the horse slightly changed his direction.

"You see," said Buller, "it won't do to sail straight across, because the current would carry us down and land us below that spot."

Mr. Podington said not a word; he expected every moment to see the horse sink into a watery grave.

"It isn't so bad after all, is it, Podington? If we had a rudder and a bit of a sail it would be a great help to the horse. This wagon is not a bad boat."

The despairing Podington looked at his feet. "It's coming in," he said in a husky voice. "Thomas, the water is over my shoes!"

"That is so," said Buller. "I am so used to water I didn't notice it.
She leaks. Do you carry anything to bail her out with?"

"Bail!" cried Podington, now finding his voice. "Oh, Thomas, we are sinking!"

"That's so," said Buller; "she leaks like a sieve."

The weight of the running-gear and of the two men was entirely too much for the buoyancy of the wagon body. The water rapidly rose toward the top of its sides.

"We are going to drown!" cried Podington, suddenly rising.

"Lick him! Lick him!" exclaimed Buller. "Make him swim faster!"

"There's nothing to lick," cried Podington, vainly lashing at the water, for he could not reach the horse's head. The poor man was dreadfully frightened; he had never even imagined it possible that he should be drowned in his own wagon.

"Whoop!" cried Buller, as the water rose over the sides. "Steady yourself, old boy, or you'll go overboard!" And the next moment the wagon body sunk out of sight.

But it did not go down very far. The deepest part of the channel of the stream had been passed, and with a bump the wheels struck the bottom.

"Heavens!" exclaimed Buller, "we are aground."

"Aground!" exclaimed Podington, "Heaven be praised!"

As the two men stood up in the submerged wagon the water was above their knees, and when Podington looked out over the surface of the pond, now so near his face, it seemed like a sheet of water he had never seen before. It was something horrible, threatening to rise and envelop him. He trembled so that he could scarcely keep his footing.

"William," said his companion, "you must sit down; if you don't, you'll tumble overboard and be drowned. There is nothing for you to hold to."

"Sit down," said Podington, gazing blankly at the water around him, "I can't do that!"

At this moment the horse made a slight movement. Having touched bottom after his efforts in swimming across the main bed of the stream, with a floating wagon in tow, he had stood for a few moments, his head and neck well above water, and his back barely visible beneath the surface. Having recovered his breath, he now thought it was time to move on.

At the first step of the horse Mr. Podington began to totter.
Instinctively he clutched Buller.

"Sit down!" cried the latter, "or you'll have us both overboard." There was no help for it; down sat Mr. Podington; and, as with a great splash he came heavily upon the seat, the water rose to his waist.

"Ough!" said he. "Thomas, shout for help."

"No use doing that," replied Buller, still standing on his nautical legs; "I don't see anybody, and I don't see any boat. We'll get out all right. Just you stick tight to the thwart."

"The what?" feebly asked the other.

"Oh, the seat, I mean. We can get to the shore all right if you steer the horse straight. Head him more across the pond."

"I can't head him," cried Podington. "I have dropped the reins!"

"Good gracious!" cried Mr. Buller, "that's bad. Can't you steer him by shouting 'Gee' and 'Haw'?"

"No," said Podington, "he isn't an ox; but perhaps I can stop him." And with as much voice as he could summon, he called out: "Whoa!" and the horse stopped.

"If you can't steer him any other way," said Buller, "we must get the reins. Lend me your whip."

"I have dropped that too," said Podington; "there it floats."

"Oh, dear," said Buller, "I guess I'll have to dive for them; if he were to run away, we should be in an awful fix."

"Don't get out! Don't get out!" exclaimed Podington. "You can reach over the dashboard."

"As that's under water," said Buller, "it will be the same thing as diving; but it's got to be done, and I'll try it. Don't you move now; I am more used to water than you are."

Mr. Buller took off his hat and asked his friend to hold it. He thought of his watch and other contents of his pockets, but there was no place to put them, so he gave them no more consideration. Then bravely getting on his knees in the water, he leaned over the dashboard, almost disappearing from sight. With his disengaged hand Mr. Podington grasped the submerged coat-tails of his friend.

In a few seconds the upper part of Mr. Buller rose from the water. He was dripping and puffing, and Mr. Podington could not but think what a difference it made in the appearance of his friend to have his hair plastered close to his head.

"I got hold of one of them," said the sputtering Buller, "but it was fast to something and I couldn't get it loose."

"Was it thick and wide?" asked Podington.

"Yes," was the answer; "it did seem so."

"Oh, that was a trace," said Podington; "I don't want that; the reins are thinner and lighter."

"Now I remember they are," said Buller. "I'll go down again."

Again Mr. Buller leaned over the dashboard, and this time he remained down longer, and when he came up he puffed and sputtered more than before.

"Is this it?" said he, holding up a strip of wet leather.

"Yes," said Podington, "you've got the reins."

"Well, take them, and steer. I would have found them sooner if his tail had not got into my eyes. That long tail's floating down there and spreading itself out like a fan; it tangled itself all around my head. It would have been much easier if he had been a bob-tailed horse."

"Now then," said Podington, "take your hat, Thomas, and I'll try to drive."

Mr. Buller put on his hat, which was the only dry thing about him, and the nervous Podington started the horse so suddenly that even the sea-legs of

Buller were surprised, and he came very near going backward into the water; but recovering himself, he sat down.

"I don't wonder you did not like to do this, William," said he. "Wet as I am, it's ghastly!"

Encouraged by his master's voice, and by the feeling of the familiar hand upon his bit, the horse moved bravely on.

But the bottom was very rough and uneven. Sometimes the wheels struck a large stone, terrifying Mr. Buller, who thought they were going to upset; and sometimes they sank into soft mud, horrifying Mr. Podington, who thought they were going to drown.

Thus proceeding, they presented a strange sight. At first Mr. Podington held his hands above the water as he drove, but he soon found this awkward, and dropped them to their usual position, so that nothing was visible above the water but the head and neck of a horse and the heads and shoulders of two men.

Now the submarine equipage came to a low place in the bottom, and even Mr. Buller shuddered as the water rose to his chin. Podington gave a howl of horror, and the horse, with high, uplifted head, was obliged to swim. At this moment a boy with a gun came strolling along the road, and hearing Mr. Podington's cry, he cast his eyes over the water. Instinctively he raised his weapon to his shoulder, and then, in an instant, perceiving that the objects he beheld were not aquatic birds, he dropped his gun and ran yelling down the road toward the mill.

But the hollow in the bottom was a narrow one, and when it was passed the depth of the water gradually decreased. The back of the horse came into view, the dashboard became visible, and the bodies and the spirits of the two men rapidly rose. Now there was vigorous splashing and tugging, and then a jet black horse, shining as if he had been newly varnished, pulled a dripping wagon containing two well-soaked men upon a shelving shore.

"Oh, I am chilled to the bones!" said Podington.

"I should think so," replied his friend; "if you have got to be wet, it is a great deal pleasanter under the water."

There was a field-road on this side of the pond which Podington well knew, and proceeding along this they came to the bridge and got into the main road.

"Now we must get home as fast as we can," cried Podington, "or we shall both take cold. I wish I hadn't lost my whip. Hi now! Get along!"

Podington was now full of life and energy, his wheels were on the hard road, and he was himself again.

When he found his head was turned toward his home, the horse set off at a great rate.

"Hi there!" cried Podington. "I am so sorry I lost my whip."

"Whip!" said Buller, holding fast to the side of the seat; "surely you don't want him to go any faster than this. And look here, William," he added, "it seems to me we are much more likely to take cold in our wet clothes if we rush through the air in this way. Really, it seems to me that horse is running away."

"Not a bit of it," cried Podington. "He wants to get home, and he wants his dinner. Isn't he a fine horse? Look how he steps out!"

"Steps out!" said Buller, "I think I'd like to step out myself. Don't you think it would be wiser for me to walk home, William? That will warm me up."

"It will take you an hour," said his friend. "Stay where you are, and
I'll have you in a dry suit of clothes in less than fifteen minutes."

"I tell you, William," said Mr. Buller, as the two sat smoking after dinner, "what you ought to do; you should never go out driving without a life-preserver and a pair of oars; I always take them. It would make you feel safer."

Mr. Buller went home the next day, because Mr. Podington's clothes did not fit him, and his own outdoor suit was so shrunken as to be uncomfortable. Besides, there was another reason, connected with the desire of horses to reach their homes, which prompted his return. But he had not forgotten his compact with his friend, and in the course of a week he wrote to Podington, inviting him to spend some days with him. Mr. Podington was a man of honor, and in spite of his recent unfortunate water experience he would not break his word. He went to Mr. Buller's seaside home at the time appointed.

Early on the morning after his arrival, before the family were up, Mr. Podington went out and strolled down to the edge of the bay. He went to look at Buller's boat. He was well aware that he would be asked to take a sail, and as Buller had driven with him, it would be impossible for him to decline sailing with Buller; but he must see the boat. There was a train for his home at a quarter past seven; if he were not on the premises he could not be asked to sail. If Buller's boat were a little, flimsy thing, he would take that train—but he would wait and see.

There was only one small boat anchored near the beach, and a man—apparently a fisherman— informed Mr. Podington that it belonged to Mr. Buller. Podington looked at it eagerly; it was not very small and not flimsy.

"Do you consider that a safe boat?" he asked the fisherman.

"Safe?" replied the man. "You could not upset her if you tried. Look at her breadth of beam! You could go anywhere in that boat! Are you thinking of buying her?"

The idea that he would think of buying a boat made Mr. Podington laugh. The information that it would be impossible to upset the little vessel had greatly cheered him, and he could laugh.

Shortly after breakfast Mr. Buller, like a nurse with a dose of medicine, came to Mr. Podington with the expected invitation to take a sail.

"Now, William," said his host, "I understand perfectly your feeling about boats, and what I wish to prove to you is that it is a feeling without any foundation. I don't want to shock you or make you nervous, so I am not going to take you out today on the bay in my boat. You are as safe on the bay as you would be on land—a little safer, perhaps, under certain circumstances, to which we will not allude— but still it is sometimes a little rough, and this, at first, might cause you some uneasiness, and so I am going to let you begin your education in the sailing line on perfectly smooth water. About three miles back of us there is a very pretty lake several miles long. It is part of the canal system which connects the town with the railroad. I have sent my boat to the town, and we can walk up there and go by the canal to the lake; it is only about three miles."

If he had to sail at all, this kind of sailing suited Mr. Podington. A canal, a quiet lake, and a boat which could not be upset. When they reached the town the boat was in the canal, ready for them.

"Now," said Mr. Buller, "you get in and make yourself comfortable. My idea is to hitch on to a canal-boat and be towed to the lake. The boats generally start about this time in the morning, and I will go and see about it."

Mr. Podington, under the direction of his friend, took a seat in the stern of the sailboat, and then he remarked:

"Thomas, have you a life-preserver on board? You know I am not used to any kind of vessel, and I am clumsy. Nothing might happen to the boat, but I might trip and fall overboard, and I can't swim."

"All right," said Buller; "here's a life-preserver, and you can put it on. I want you to feel perfectly safe. Now I will go and see about the tow."

But Mr. Buller found that the canal-boats would not start at their usual time; the loading of one of them was not finished, and he was informed that he might have to wait for an hour or more. This did not suit Mr. Buller at all, and he did not hesitate to show his annoyance.

"I tell you, sir, what you can do," said one of the men in charge of the boats; "if you don't want to wait till we are ready to start, we'll let you have a boy and a horse to tow you up to the lake. That won't cost you much, and they'll be back before we want 'em."

The bargain was made, and Mr. Buller joyfully returned to his boat with the intelligence that they were not to wait for the canal-boats. A long rope, with a horse attached to the other end of it, was speedily made fast to the boat, and with a boy at the head of the horse, they started up the canal.

"Now this is the kind of sailing I like," said Mr. Podington. "If I lived near a canal I believe I would buy a boat and train my horse to tow. I could have a long pair of rope-lines and drive him myself; then when the roads were rough and bad the canal would always be smooth."

"This is all very nice," replied Mr. Buller, who sat by the tiller to keep the boat away from the bank, "and I am glad to see you in a boat under any circumstances. Do you know, William, that although I did not plan it, there could not have been a better way to begin your sailing education. Here we glide along, slowly and gently, with no possible thought of danger, for if the boat should suddenly spring a leak, as if it were the body of a wagon, all we would have to do would be to step on shore, and by the time you get to the end of the canal you will like this gentle motion so much that you will be perfectly ready to begin the second stage of your nautical education."

"Yes," said Mr. Podington. "How long did you say this canal is?"

"About three miles," answered his friend. "Then we will go into the lock and in a few minutes we shall be on the lake."

"So far as I am concerned," said Mr. Podington, "I wish the canal were twelve miles long. I cannot imagine anything pleasanter than this. If I lived anywhere near a canal—a long canal, I mean, this one is too short—I'd—"

"Come, come now," interrupted Buller. "Don't be content to stay in the primary school just because it is easy. When we get on the lake I will show you that in a boat, with a gentle breeze, such as we are likely to have today, you will find the motion quite as pleasing, and ever so much more inspiriting. I should not be a bit surprised, William, if after you have been two or three times on the lake you will ask me—yes, positively ask me—to take you out on the bay!"

Mr. Podington smiled, and leaning backward, he looked up at the beautiful blue sky.

"You can't give me anything better than this, Thomas," said he; "but you needn't think I am weakening; you drove with me, and I will sail with you."

The thought came into Buller's mind that he had done both of these things with Podington, but he did not wish to call up unpleasant memories, and said nothing.

About half a mile from the town there stood a small cottage where house-cleaning was going on, and on a fence, not far from the canal, there hung a carpet gaily adorned with stripes and spots of red and yellow.

When the drowsy tow-horse came abreast of the house, and the carpet caught his eye, he suddenly stopped and gave a start toward the canal. Then, impressed with a horror of the glaring apparition, he gathered himself up, and with a bound dashed along the tow-path. The astounded boy gave a shout, but was speedily left behind. The boat of Mr. Buller shot forward as if she had been struck by a squall.

The terrified horse sped on as if a red and yellow demon were after him. The boat bounded, and plunged, and frequently struck the grassy bank of the canal, as if it would break itself to pieces. Mr. Podington clutched the boom to keep himself from being thrown out, while Mr. Buller, both hands upon the tiller, frantically endeavored to keep the boat from the bank.

"William!" he screamed, "he is running away with us; we shall be dashed to pieces! Can't you get forward and cast off that line?"

"What do you mean?" cried Podington, as the boom gave a great jerk as if it would break its fastenings and drag him overboard.

"I mean untie the tow-line. We'll be smashed if you don't! I can't leave this tiller. Don't try to stand up; hold on to the boom and creep forward. Steady now, or you'll be overboard!"

Mr. Podington stumbled to the bow of the boat, his efforts greatly impeded by the big cork life-preserver tied under his arms, and the motion of the boat was so violent and erratic that he was obliged to hold on to the mast with one arm and to try to loosen the knot with the other; but there was a great strain on the rope, and he could do nothing with one hand.

"Cut it! Cut it!" cried Mr. Buller.

"I haven't a knife," replied Podington.

Mr. Buller was terribly frightened; his boat was cutting through the water as never vessel of her class had sped since sail-boats were invented, and bumping against the bank as if she were a billiard-ball rebounding from the edge of a table. He forgot he was in a boat; he only knew that for the first time in his life he was in a runaway. He let go the tiller. It was of no use to him.

"William," he cried, "let us jump out the next time we are near enough to shore!"

"Don't do that! Don't do that!" replied Podington. "Don't jump out in a runaway; that is the way to get hurt. Stick to your seat, my boy; he can't keep this up much longer. He'll lose his wind!"

Mr. Podington was greatly excited, but he was not frightened, as Buller was. He had been in a runaway before, and he could not help thinking how much better a wagon was than a boat in such a case.

"If he were hitched up shorter and I had a snaffle-bit and a stout pair of reins," thought he, "I could soon bring him up."

But Mr. Buller was rapidly losing his wits. The horse seemed to be going faster than ever. The boat bumped harder against the bank, and at one time Buller thought they could turn over.

Suddenly a thought struck him.

"William," he shouted, "tip that anchor over the side! Throw it in, any way!"

Mr. Podington looked about him, and, almost under his feet, saw the anchor. He did not instantly comprehend why Buller wanted it thrown overboard, but this was not a time to ask questions. The difficulties imposed by the life-preserver, and the necessity of holding on with one hand, interfered very much with his getting at the anchor and throwing it over the side, but at last he succeeded, and just as the boat threw up her bow as if she were about to jump on shore, the anchor went out and its line shot after it. There was an irregular trembling of the boat as the anchor struggled along the bottom of the canal; then there was a great shock; the boat ran into the bank and stopped; the tow-line was tightened like a guitar-string, and the horse, jerked back with great violence, came tumbling in a heap upon the ground.

Instantly Mr. Podington was on the shore and running at the top of his speed toward the horse. The astounded animal had scarcely begun to struggle to his feet when Podington rushed upon him, pressed his head back to the ground, and sat upon it.

"Hurrah!" he cried, waving his hat above his head. "Get out, Buller; he is all right now!"

Presently Mr. Buller approached, very much shaken up.

"All right?" he said. "I don't call a horse flat in a road with a man on his head all right; but hold him down till we get him loose from my boat. That is the thing to do. William, cast him loose from the boat before you let him up! What will he do when he gets up?"

"Oh. he'll be quiet enough when he gets up," said Podington. "But if you've got a knife you can cut his traces—-I mean that rope—but no, you needn't. Here comes the boy. We'll settle this business in very short order now."

When the horse was on his feet, and all connection between the animal and the boat had been severed, Mr. Podington looked at his friend.

"Thomas," said he, "you seem to have had a hard time of it. You have lost your hat and you look as if you had been in a wrestling-match."

"I have," replied the other; "I wrestled with that tiller and I wonder it didn't throw me out."

Now approached the boy. "Shall I hitch him on again, sir?" said he.
"He's quiet enough now."

"No," cried Mr. Buller; "I want no more sailing after a horse, and, besides, we can't go on the lake with that boat; she has been battered about so much that she must have opened a dozen seams. The best thing we can do is to walk home."

Mr. Podington agreed with his friend that walking home was the best thing they could do. The boat was examined and found to be leaking, but not very badly, and when her mast had been unshipped and everything had been made tight and right on board, she was pulled out of the way of tow-lines and boats, and made fast until she could be sent for from the town.

Mr. Buller and Mr. Podington walked back toward the town. They had not gone very far when they met a party of boys, who, upon seeing them, burst into unseemly laughter.

"Mister," cried one of them, "you needn't be afraid of tumbling into the canal. Why don't you take off your life-preserver and let that other man put it on his head?"

The two friends looked at each other and could not help joining in the laughter of the boys.

"By George! I forgot all about this," said Podington, as he unfastened the cork jacket. "It does look a little super-timid to wear a life-preserver just because one happens to be walking by the side of a canal."

Mr. Buller tied a handkerchief on his head, and Mr. Podington rolled up his life-preserver and carried it under his arm. Thus they reached the town, where Buller bought a hat, Podington dispensed with his bundle, and arrangements were made to bring back the boat.

"Runaway in a sailboat!" exclaimed one of the canal boatmen when he had heard about the accident. "Upon my word! That beats anything that could happen to a man!"

"No, it doesn't," replied Mr. Buller, quietly. "I have gone to the bottom in a foundered road-wagon."

The man looked at him fixedly.

"Was you ever struck in the mud in a balloon?" he asked.

"Not yet," replied Mr. Buller.

It required ten days to put Mr. Buller's sailboat into proper condition, and for ten days Mr. Podington stayed with his friend, and enjoyed his visit very much. They strolled on the beach, they took long walks in the back country, they fished from the end of a pier, they smoked, they talked, and were happy and content.

"Thomas," said Mr. Podington, on the last evening of his stay, "I have enjoyed myself very much since I have been down here, and now, Thomas, if I were to come down again next summer, would you mind— would you mind, not——"

"I would not mind it a bit," replied Buller, promptly. "I'll never so much as mention it; so you can come along without a thought of it. And since you have alluded to the subject, William," he continued, "I'd like very much to come and see you again; you know my visit was a very short one this year. That is a beautiful country you live in. Such a variety of scenery, such an opportunity for walks and rambles! But, William, if you could only make up your mind not to——"

"Oh, that is all right!" exclaimed Podington. "I do not need to make up my mind. You come to my house and you will never so much as hear of it. Here's my hand upon it!"

"And here's mine!" said Mr. Buller.

And they shook hands over a new compact.

End of the book.